CARBOHYDRATES

WRITTEN BY
E.C. ANDREWS

PowerKiDS press

Published in 2025
by The Rosen Publishing Group, Inc.
2544 Clinton Street, Buffalo, NY 14224

© 2024 BookLife Publishing Ltd.

Written by: E.C. Andrews
Edited by: Elise Carraway
Designed by: Jasmine Pointer

Cataloging-in-Publication Data

Names: Andrews, E.C.
Title: Carbohydrates / E.C. Andrews.
Description: Buffalo, NY : PowerKids Press, 2025. | Series: Fantastic foods | Includes glossary and index.
Identifiers: ISBN 9781499449136 (pbk.) | ISBN 9781499449143 (library bound) | ISBN 9781499449150 (ebook)
Subjects: LCSH: Bread--Juvenile literature. | Grain--Juvenile literature. | Carbohydrates--Juvenile literature.
Classification: LCC TX769.A537 2025 | DDC 641.8'15--dc23

All rights reserved.

No part of this book may be reproduced in any form without permission in writing from the publisher, except by a reviewer.

Manufactured in the United States of America
CPSIA Compliance Information: Batch #CW25PK. For further information contact Rosen Publishing at 1-800-237-9932.

Find us on

Image Credits

All images are courtesy of Shutterstock.com. With thanks to Getty Images, Thinkstock Photo and iStockphoto.

Cover – grey_and, thaikrit, Galyna Syngaievska, Natthapol Siridech, Amarita, marilyn barbone, Yeti studio. 4–5 – Africa Studio, New Africa. 6–7 – popcorner, nehophoto. 8–9 – nednapa, Ihor Hvozdetskyi, lovelyday12, allstars. 10–11 – Tanya Sid, bigacis. 12–13 – beats1, Paulo Vilela. 14–15 – Dima Aslanian, Africa Studio. 16–17 – Sea Wave, Plateresca. 18–19 – nednapa, Brent Hofacker, MariaKovaleva. 20–21 – marilyn barbone, Daisy Daisy. 22–23 – StockImageFactory.com.

CONTENTS

Page 4	Daily Diet
Page 6	What Are Carbohydrates?
Page 8	Where to Find Carbohydrates
Page 10	Grains
Page 12	Whole Grains
Page 14	Bread
Page 16	Pasta
Page 18	Potatoes
Page 20	Healthy Carbohydrates
Page 22	Perfect Plate
Page 24	Glossary and Index

Words that look like this can be found in the glossary on page 24.

Daily Diet

Have you ever heard of carbohydrates? Do you know why we should eat them? Maybe you are asking yourself why it even matters. So long as you eat enough food, who cares what kinds of foods you have?

We all need to eat enough different foods to keep our bodies healthy. This is called having a balanced diet. Carbohydrates are a very important part of a balanced diet. Let's talk about why!

Your diet is the kinds of foods you usually eat.

WHAT Are CARBOHYDRATES?

Carbohydrates help give your body enough <u>energy</u> to do all the jobs it needs to do. Starch is one kind of carbohydrate. Carbohydrates can be found in many different foods.

Foods made with carbohydrates have high amounts of fiber. Fiber helps you feel full. Some of these foods have lots of <u>vitamins</u> in them. Your body needs different kinds of vitamins to work properly.

WHERE to FIND CARBOHYDRATES

Carbohydrates come from some plants. Many vegetables have small amounts of starch in them. Certain vegetables, such as potatoes, corn, and beans, have much higher amounts of starch. These are called starchy foods.

Grains are another kind of carbohydrate. Grains are the <u>edible</u> seeds that come from different types of grasses. The seeds are where plants store a lot of energy.

BARLEY

GRAINS

FLOUR

WHEAT

Oats and wheat are grains. Some grains are used to make flour, which goes into cakes and bread. To make flour, the grain is dried and ground up into powder.

Grains and grain flour can be used to make lots of different foods, such as bread, pasta, and breakfast cereals. Some grains need to be cooked before they can be eaten.

BREAKFAST CEREAL

WHOLE GRAINS

Whole grains are grains that have not been processed. This means they have not been changed or had anything taken away from them. Whole grains that haven't been processed keep a lot more of their fiber.

Whole grain bread makes delicious sandwiches!

WHOLE GRAIN PASTA

Whole grains are also full of vitamins that are good for your body. Eating foods made with whole grains is a good way to keep your diet balanced and healthy.

BREAD

The main ingredient in bread is flour. Flour is a powder that is made from ground-up grains. Most flour is made from wheat. Bread can be used in lots of different <u>recipes</u>.

Whole wheat bread is made with whole grains, which add healthy fiber, <u>protein,</u> and vitamins to your diet. Eating whole wheat bread can help you feel healthier by boosting your energy levels.

PASTA

Like bread, pasta is a carbohydrate made with flour. Whole wheat pasta is also a <u>source</u> of fiber. Pasta can be made into all kinds of shapes.

Lots of different things can be added to pasta, such as vegetables and meats. This makes it a great food for helping you keep your diet balanced.

POTATOES

Potatoes are a type of root vegetable. Root vegetables are vegetables that grow underground. Even though they do not come from grains, they are still carbohydrates.

Other root vegetables are carbohydrates too.

Like pasta, potatoes can be used in lots of different ways. They can be eaten with other foods and used in many different recipes. Potato skins are full of healthy fiber.

BAKED POTATO

POTATO SALAD

Healthy Carbohydrates

Carbohydrates that are made from whole grains can be made into many healthy and tasty things. However, some carbohydrates have extra things added to them that can affect how balanced your diet is.

Foods such as cakes, muffins, and cookies are all carbohydrates that have a lot of added sugar. A small amount of sugar in your diet is normal, but it is easy to get too much.

Healthy eating is all about balance!

PERFECT PLATE

Carbohydrates are in a lot of things. These foods are an important part of your diet. Eating enough carbohydrates will help give your body the energy it needs to work properly.

Which fantastic foods are your favorites?

Here are some kinds of different kinds of foods that can be eaten alongside carbohydrates as part of a balanced diet:

MEAT AND FISH

MILK AND DAIRY

FRUITS AND VEGETABLES

CARBOHYDRATES (ENERGY FOODS)

Which of these foods would be on your perfect plate?

Glossary

edible	able to be eaten
energy	the power that makes living things able to move and live
protein	a substance that is important in growing and mending the body
recipes	instructions on how to make certain types of food or meals
source	where something comes from
vitamins	substances needed for normal and healthy growth

Index

bread 10–12, 14–16
energy 6, 9, 15, 22
fiber 7, 12, 15–16, 19
flour 10–11, 14, 16
pasta 11, 13, 16–17, 19
recipes 14, 19
vegetables 8, 17–18, 23
wheat 10, 14, 16